D0860356

DECISIVE
BATTLES

WORLD WAR II

DECISIVE BATTLES

MICHAEL GALLAGHER

SEA-TO-SEA

Mankato Collingwood London

Designer Jason Billin
Editor Sarah Ridley
Art Director Jonathan Hair
Editor-in-Chief John C. Miles
Picture research Diana Morris

Picture credits
AP/Topham: 21
Cody Images: 8b, 10b, 11, 12b, 16b,
19, 28, 29, 31, 32 Picturepoint/Topham:
front cover t, back cover t, 1, 9, 17, 23,
24b, 25, 27, 30
Roger-Viollet/Topham: 18b
Topham: front cover b, back cover b,
7, 15, 26b

*Every attempt has been made to clear
copyright. Should there be any inadvertent
omission please apply to the publisher for
rectification.*

Note to parents and teachers:
Every effort has been made by the Publishers
to ensure that the web sites in this book are
suitable for children, that they are of the
highest educational value, and that they
contain no inappropriate or offensive
material. However, because of the nature of
the Internet, it is impossible to guarantee
that the contents of these sites will not be
altered. We strongly advise that Internet
access be supervised by a responsible adult.

This edition first published in 2009 by
Sea-to-Sea Publications
Distributed by Black Rabbit Books
P.O. Box 3263
Mankato, Minnesota 56002

Copyright © Sea-to-Sea Publications 2009

Printed in China

All rights reserved.

Library of Congress Cataloging-in-Publication Data:

Gallagher, Michael.
  Decisive battles / Michael Gallagher.
    p. cm. -- (World War Two)
  Includes index.
  Summary: "Describes battles that marked turning points in World War II, such as
the Bliztkrieg on Poland, Pearl Harbor, D-Day, and more"--Provided by publisher.
  ISBN 978-1-59771-139-5
  1. World War, 1939-1945--Campaigns--Juvenile literature. I. Title.
  D743.7.G35 2009
  940.54'2--dc22
                                        2008007829

9 8 7 6 5 4 3 2

Published by arrangement with the Watts Publishing
Group Ltd, London.

CONTENTS

Chamberlain and appeasement

Like many of his generation, British Prime Minister Neville Chamberlain recalled with horror the bloodshed of World War I, and strove to avoid its repetition. Chamberlain therefore adopted a policy of "appeasement." In return for peace assurances, he accepted Hitler's demands, notably, the occupation of Czechoslovakia's Sudetenland region in 1938. Ultimately, Germany's continued aggression forced a reluctant Chamberlain into declaring war on September 3, 1939. He was succeeded as prime minister by Winston Churchill in 1940.

Hitler's Racist Dream

World War Two began as a European war in which Nazi Germany was the main aggressor. The Nazis, led by Adolf Hitler, insisted that Germans were biologically superior to all other peoples—especially the Jews. Their aim was to end the humiliation of Germany's defeat in World War I, and expand German *Lebensraum* (living space) through a ruthless conquest of eastern Europe and the Soviet Union. These lands—stripped of their native population— would be the heart of a new, and supposedly pure, Nazi empire.

Axis of Evil

Germany's main European ally was Italy, led by the fascist dictator, Benito Mussolini. Like the Nazis, the Fascists were authoritarian and militaristic. They also hated communism and wanted to acquire colonies. However, they did not share the Nazis' obsession with race. The German-Italian partnership was called the Axis. Japan joined the Axis in 1940, but its ambition was to conquer an empire in Asia. This brought conflict with the United States after 1941, making the war truly global.

Battle Zones

The Axis powers were opposed by the Allied countries, which eventually included Britain and its empire, the United States, the Soviet Union, and a number of smaller forces. With such diverse participants, the big battles of World War II took place in no fewer than four principal regions. On Europe's Eastern Front, the Soviet Union struggled against Hitler's racist expansion plan.
On the Western Front, Britain, the United States and others fought off German aggression, and later launched their own offensives to defeat Hitler. In North Africa and the Mediterranean, the Allies fought both German and Italian forces, before invading Italy and trying to attack Germany from the south. Last but not least, the U.S., Britain, Australia, and others engaged Japan in a long and bloodthirsty war across the vast Pacific Ocean region.

Battles and Casualties

Big battles were dramatic moments that often helped change the course of World War II, but they were not responsible for most deaths. The war became a "total war" that spread far beyond the battlefield. Cities and industry were bombed from the air and this, combined with atrocities against civilians, meant civilian deaths far exceeded those of the various armies. Most notoriously, at least six million died in Hitler's attempt to exterminate Europe's Jews.

German dictator Adolf Hitler (right) poses with Italian leader Benito Mussolini before the war.

The road to war

September 18, 1931 Japan launches attack on Manchuria, northern China.

January 30, 1933 Hitler becomes Chancellor of Germany.

October 3, 1935 Italy invades Abyssinia (Ethiopia).

July 7, 1937 Japan begins invasion of China.

March 15, 1939 Germans enter Czechoslovakia beyond the Sudetenland.

May 22, 1939 Military alliance between Germany and Italy.

September 1, 1939 Germany invades Poland.

December 7, 1941 Japan attacks U.S. fleet at Pearl Harbor.

Blitzkrieg on Poland

Germany's invasion of Poland in September 1939 began the war in Europe. Yet this was no ordinary attack. The Nazis overwhelmed their enemy with a ferocious new military tactic.

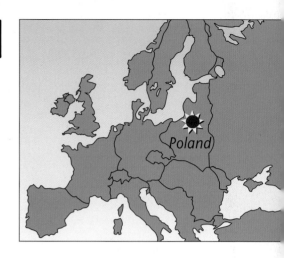

Poland

The Junkers Ju87 ("Stuka") dive bomber

Ugly and terrifying, the Ju87 became a symbol of Nazi blitzkrieg. Designed to be used alongside ground forces, it could deliver its 1,100lb (500kg) single bomb, or four smaller bombs, with lethal accuracy. Complete with special sirens that screamed as it swooped to attack, its very appearance could be enough to destroy enemy morale.

Hitler's Gamble

A key part of Hitler's plan for expanding Germany was the conquest of Poland which, since World War I, had divided Germany from its province of East Prussia. Hitler wrongly assumed that Britain and France—whose appeasement policies had allowed him to rearm for several years—would once again do nothing to stop him. On September 1, 1939, he launched a sudden invasion of Poland using a new strategy called *Blitzkrieg* (lightning war).

Death in a Flash

Blitzkrieg came first of all from the sky. Without warning, German aircraft launched shock raids on Polish communications and military installations. Tanks and infantry rapidly followed, smashing through the static Polish defenses before turning to attack them from behind. Despite mounting a brave resistance, the Polish military was outdated, and no match for this kind of warfare. Within days its troop formations were cut to pieces and then encircled by the fast-moving invaders.

"*Take a good look around Warsaw. That is how I can deal with any European city.***"**

Adolf Hitler, October 1939

Warsaw under attack on September 1, 1939 as Germany invades Poland.

The Atrocities Begin

The blitzkrieg also bombarded fleeing refugees, creating chaos along major roads. Even behind the front line, the Nazis started persecuting civilians, especially Polish Jews.

Partners in Crime

The invasion was assisted by an agreement between Germany and Poland's eastern neighbor, the Soviet Union. The two sides secretly plotted to cut Poland in two and share the spoils. Within ten days, Warsaw surrendered to the Germans, and Poland effectively ceased to exist. The lightning war had killed up to 70,000 of its servicemen, and captured ten times as many. Now, blitzkrieg would be applied against France, the Netherlands and Norway, and, ultimately, against the Soviet Union.

Smash and grab in Europe, 1939–40

August 23, 1939 Berlin and Moscow agree nonaggression pact.

September 1 Germany invades Poland.

September 3 Britain and France declare war on Germany.

April 9, 1940 Germany invades Denmark and Norway.

May 10 Germany invades Belgium, the Netherlands, and Luxemburg.

May 27 Britain forced to evacuate troops from Dunkirk, France.

June 14 Germans enter Paris.

The Battle of Britain

In order to concentrate on Germany's eastward expansion, Hitler needed peace in the west. When Britain ruled this out, he began a massive and sustained airborne attack.

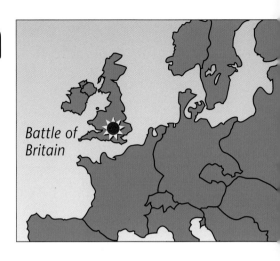

Battle of Britain

Radar: Britain's sixth sense

Radar detects faraway objects by transmitting radio waves and measuring the time taken for the signal to bounce back. In 1940 it was a new invention, and helped Britain by warning of incoming German squadrons. The RAF could then launch a surprise attack, despite having fewer aircraft of its own. Though Germany developed its own radar, the Allies maintained a technical edge throughout the war.

Britain Alone

After France surrendered in 1940, Hitler assumed the British would make peace, but that summer they held firm under a new and determined leader, Winston Churchill. With the United States and the Soviet Union yet to enter the war on its side, Britain now stood alone, awaiting the inevitable invasion of its own shores.

Unequal Battle

Surrounded by sea, Britain was hard to invade, so Hitler used his air force, the *Luftwaffe*, to try and overcome the Royal Air Force (RAF) air defenses first. The Luftwaffe leader, Hermann Goering, assumed that, because the RAF's Fighter Command unit was greatly outnumbered, it would soon collapse. But his own fighter planes were at the limits of their range, and could only remain in battle for short periods before they had to return to base for refueling. The British also had a new invention—radar (see panel left)—to help them. And, they were able to build aircraft at a faster rate than the Germans could shoot them down.

Miraculous Escape

Even so, by the end of August, Fighter Command had lost much of its strength, and defeat seemed likely. What saved Britain was Hitler's temper. Enraged at a British air raid on Berlin and unaware of how close he was to victory, he switched his attack to bombing British cities. These raids would continue for many months, killing thousands of civilians. Yet they gave Fighter Command time to recover, and then to hit back. In September, amid heavy losses, Hitler called off his planned invasion of Britain.

Heroes of the Air

The skill and heroism of RAF fighter pilots was a key factor in Britain's victory in the Battle of Britain. However, not every pilot was actually British. Pilots from the British Empire, as well as Poles and Czechs, whose own countries the Nazis had overwhelmed, also fought. Churchill said of them: "Never in the field of human conflict has so much been owed by so many to so few."

Britain alone, 1940

June 22 France accepts German surrender terms.

July 10 Germany begins attacking British ports and shipping.

August 1 Hitler announces intention to destroy the RAF.

August 26 British bombing raid on Berlin.

September 7 Luftwaffe begins retaliatory attacks on British cities. Continues until May 1941.

September 17 Hitler postpones Operation Sealion, his planned invasion of Britain.

❝Hitler knows that he will have to break us in this island or lose the war.❞

Winston Churchill, June 18, 1940

A German airplane, crashed in a field in 1940, is guarded by a British soldier.

The Battle of the Atlantic

Being an island, Britain depended on cargo from across the Atlantic Ocean for its survival. But German submarines, known as U-boats, threatened this lifeline, almost to destruction.

Battle of the Atlantic

U-boats: danger from the deep

German *Unterseeboots* (submarines) would typically spend 90 percent of their time on the surface, where their diesel engines outpaced the ships they attacked. Below water, they used battery power and were much slower, though still deadly. Later versions were able to travel underwater faster and for much longer. By 1943 however, the U-boat threat was much diminished.

An Island Besieged

The Battle of the Atlantic was an attempt to starve Britain into submission by preventing imports of food, arms, and other essentials being delivered. At first, there were only a few U-boats. But in 1940, when the Germans captured submarine bases in occupied Europe, the threat grew. Merchant ships traveled in convoys (groups) for safety, but were still easy targets for the U-boats, which hunted in "wolfpacks," often at night. In the last half of 1940 alone, some three million tons of Atlantic shipping was lost. The Germans referred to this as their "happy time."

U.S. Assistance

Despite official neutrality, the United States gave Britain 50 old destroyers to help defend itself, in exchange for British bases in the Caribbean. The U.S. Navy also began escorting merchant ships. In October 1941 the American destroyer *Reuben James* was sunk by a torpedo with the loss of more than 100 lives. Even when the U.S. entered the war on Britain's side, the U-boat peril continued. At first, the Americans failed to maintain blackouts and radio silence at sea, with the result that, in 1942, the Germans sank around 500 ships off the U.S. and Caribbean coasts—another "happy time."

> **"** *The outcome of the war depends on the success or failure of the Battle of the Atlantic.* **"**
>
> German Admiral Karl Doenitz

The Tide Turns

Ultimately, however, the Germans could not destroy Allied ships faster than American dockyards could replace them. New technology, including long-range aircraft and antisubmarine weapons, also helped reduce the U-boat threat. But the biggest reason for Allied victory in the Atlantic was intelligence. Once the Allies had deciphered Germany's ENIGMA military communication code (see panel), they could avoid attacks. In fact, they were increasingly able to sink German U-boats so that, by the spring of 1943, the battle was effectively over. At least 75,000 Allied seamen had lost their lives.

A group of German U-boats in dock.

War in the Atlantic, 1939–42

September 3, 1939 British liner *Athenia* sunk on day one of the war.

August 17, 1940 Hitler proclaims total blockade of British shipping.

Jan–March 1942 Second German "happy time" off the Americas.

February 1, 1942 Germans change their ENIGMA code, denying Allies U-boat intelligence.

June 1942 Record Allied shipping losses.

30 October 1942 British retrieve the ENIGMA code from U-559. Allied losses quickly diminish.

Vital intelligence— the ENIGMA code

In October 1942, three British naval personnel entered a sinking German U-boat and in doing so, changed the course of the Atlantic conflict. Lt. Tony Fasson, Able Seaman Colin Grazier, and Canteen Assistant Tommy Brown managed to retrieve the vessel's ENIGMA machine, enabling British intelligence to crack the German navy's secret communication code. Brown and Grazier went down with the submarine, but all three men were awarded the George Cross for their actions.

Pearl Harbor

At Pearl Harbor, Japan made an enemy of the United States. Now, the world's most powerful country would enter the war.

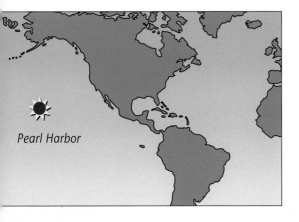

Pearl Harbor

Japan's Dilemma

Hitler's Germany was not the only aggressor of World War II. In Asia, Japan was terrorizing its neighbors, especially China. But Japan had a problem: to expand its empire it needed to capture raw materials from countries such as modernday Malaysia. To do this, it had to eliminate any potential opposition in the Pacific Ocean. The solution was a surprise attack on the U.S. Pacific Fleet, anchored at Pearl Harbor in Hawaii.

Careful Planning

The brains behind the operation was Japan's naval commander, Isoroku Yamamoto. He was convinced that, with new long-range aircraft carriers, he could destroy the American ships in one devastating raid. Yamamoto assembled the most powerful carrier force ever, with more than 400 planes plus submarines and battleships. On December 7, 1941, they attacked.

Vicious Onslaught

The attacks were rapid and lethal. U.S. airfields around Pearl Harbor were wrecked, along with nearly 200 aircraft on the ground. Around 2,400 servicemen were killed or wounded. And, in just two hours, the Japanese sank no fewer than five battleships and damaged 16 other vessels. For months afterward, the U.S. Navy was too weak to stop the Japanese advance through the Pacific.

U.S. isolationism

Isolationism was the U.S.'s policy to stay out of European conflicts. It was popular in the late 1930s, and meant the US maintained neutrality when war first broke out in 1939, though President Roosevelt still helped Britain with their war effort. After Pearl Harbor, most Americans supported war against Japan. However, Roosevelt made defeating Germany the bigger priority.

U.S. battleships ablaze and sinking after two waves of Japanese aircraft had attacked Pearl Harbor.

Mixed Results

Even so, Pearl Harbor did not achieve everything Yamamoto had hoped for. Three U.S. aircraft carriers were elsewhere and so survived, and all but three of the ships that were hit were repaired over time. The Japanese could have inflicted a greater blow by wrecking dockyards and fuel reserves. In fact, in the long run, Pearl Harbor backfired, for it ensured an outraged USA entered the war, an opponent that Japan would fail to defeat.

❝ *Since the unprovoked and dastardly attack by Japan on Sunday, December 7th, a state of war has existed between the United States and the Japanese Empire.* **❞**

President Franklin D. Roosevelt, December 8, 1941

War on the USA, 1941

July 23 Japan occupies southern Indochina. U.S. trade embargo.

November 26 U.S. demands Japanese withdrawal from China and Indochina.

December 7 Japanese attack U.S. Pacific Fleet at Pearl Harbor. Simultaneous attacks on Guam, Wake, Philippines, Malaya, and Hong Kong.

December 8 U.S. declares war on Japan.

December 11 Germany declares war on U.S.

The Battle of Midway

At Midway Island, the U.S. Navy avoided a Japanese ambush, overcame superior enemy strength, and helped turn the tide of the Pacific conflict.

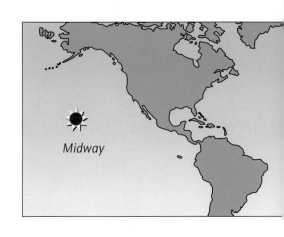

Midway

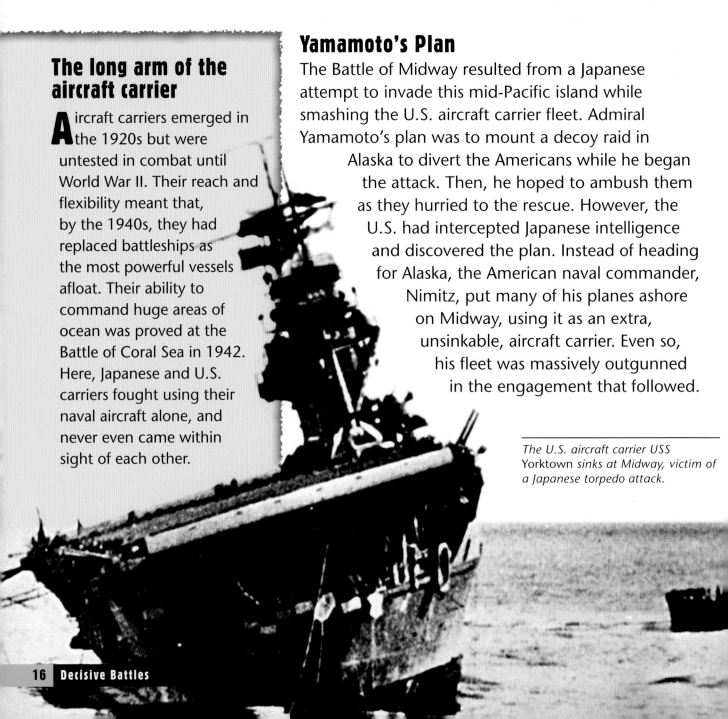

The long arm of the aircraft carrier

Aircraft carriers emerged in the 1920s but were untested in combat until World War II. Their reach and flexibility meant that, by the 1940s, they had replaced battleships as the most powerful vessels afloat. Their ability to command huge areas of ocean was proved at the Battle of Coral Sea in 1942. Here, Japanese and U.S. carriers fought using their naval aircraft alone, and never even came within sight of each other.

Yamamoto's Plan

The Battle of Midway resulted from a Japanese attempt to invade this mid-Pacific island while smashing the U.S. aircraft carrier fleet. Admiral Yamamoto's plan was to mount a decoy raid in Alaska to divert the Americans while he began the attack. Then, he hoped to ambush them as they hurried to the rescue. However, the U.S. had intercepted Japanese intelligence and discovered the plan. Instead of heading for Alaska, the American naval commander, Nimitz, put many of his planes ashore on Midway, using it as an extra, unsinkable, aircraft carrier. Even so, his fleet was massively outgunned in the engagement that followed.

The U.S. aircraft carrier USS Yorktown sinks at Midway, victim of a Japanese torpedo attack.

First Exchanges

On June 3, 1942 the battle began as a massive Japanese armada advanced on Midway. The Japanese were shocked to find American ships already in position as they approached, and a first wave of U.S. planes attempted their own ambush. However, this did little damage, and the Japanese launched their own raids against Midway's airfields. Again, these failed to make a breakthrough, and U.S. planes remained able to refuel on the island.

> **" They had no right to win, yet they did. "**
>
> *Walter Lord, U.S. historian*

Lucky Strike

Some of the American planes became separated from the others and got lost. But one squadron of torpedo-bombers did reach the Japanese fleet. These were almost entirely destroyed by Japanese "Zero" fighters. Yet, in an extraordinary piece of good luck, a group of American dive-bombers, previously lost, came across the scene of action. With the defending planes otherwise engaged, the high-flying dive-bombers had perfect targets. Within minutes, three of the huge Japanese carriers were ablaze.

A Heavy Price

Other clashes followed, but the Japanese had lost the initiative. In total, Midway cost them four aircraft carriers, a heavy cruiser, and hundreds of planes. Thousands of men were killed. In exchange, the Americans lost one carrier and 130 planes. One hundred American servicemen died. The Japanese navy would never fully recover.

Midway, 1942

April 18 Planes from U.S. aircraft carrier, *Hornet*, bomb Japan. Japanese determined to destroy U.S. carrier fleet.

June 3 First engagement as Japanese approach Midway Island.

June 4 U.S. dive bombers sink three Japanese aircraft carriers. Fourth carrier later sunk.

June 6 Americans sink Japanese cruiser.

June 7 American aircraft carrier, USS *Yorktown*, torpedoed and sunk.

Japanese Admiral Yamamoto

El Alamein

The early years of World War II were tough for the Allies. El Alamein raised spirits and proved that, in the right conditions, even the mighty German army could be beaten.

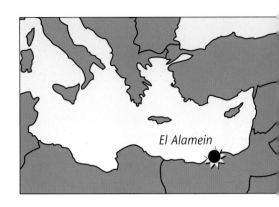

El Alamein

Monty vs. the Desert Fox

Considered vain, stubborn, and even rude, "Monty" liked to do things his own way. Nevertheless, he was loved by his troops, whose welfare he always tried to protect. After El Alamein he fought in Italy and Normandy, and accepted the formal German surrender in May 1945.

His opponent at El Alamein, Field Marshal Erwin Rommel, was known as the "Desert Fox" and was one of the most respected German generals of the war. His Afrika Korps went on the offensive, pushing British forces into Egypt from Libya before their advance was finally halted at El Alamein.

Britain Demoralized

Since 1940, the Germans had inflicted a series of defeats on British forces in the North African desert, and Britain feared losing control of Egypt, the Suez Canal, and the sea route to India. Amid this anxiety, Bernard "Monty" Montgomery was appointed commander of the British 8th Army in August 1942. Montgomery would not hear of defeat, and boosted his troops' morale. After rebuffing the latest German offensive, he began building a force to counter-attack. This would take place near El Alamein, Egypt.

"Monty" in his command tank.

British troops capture a German tank in the North African desert.

Montgomery's Caution

The German commander, Rommel, was already at the very limits of his supply lines, and he was soon outnumbered in both men and weapons. To Rommel's 500 tanks, Montgomery eventually had 1,000. Even so, Montgomery waited until he felt ready to strike, constructing dummy tanks and pipelines to confuse the Germans.

Spearhead through the Mines

The moment for action came on the night of October 23. In an initial phase, codenamed Operation Lightfoot, Montgomery ordered a heavy bombardment. Then, he sent in infantry to create pathways through Rommel's defensive minefields. This part of the battle resulted in heavy casualties for Montgomery. However, in the second phase, codenamed Operation Supercharge, his tanks managed to hold on long enough to get reinforcements through. By early November, they had driven a wedge between the Germans and their Italian allies, sending both into retreat. Axis forces lost 30,000 men between them and, later, Rommel's entire army would be captured.

> **❝ A victory at last. How good it is for the nerves. ❞**
>
> *King George VI*

War in the desert, 1942–3

May 26-7 1942 British retreat to El Alamein.

June 21, 1942 Surrender of Allied forces at Tobruk, Libya.

August 30, 1942 Montgomery repels German attack at Alam Halfa.

October 23, 1942 Second Battle of El Alamein begins.

November 4, 1942 Rommel sent into retreat.

November 8, 1942 Operation Torch: British and U.S. troops land in French North Africa.

May 13, 1943 Rommel's successor, Arnim, surrenders in Tunisia.

Guadalcanal

After months of responding to Japanese attacks in the Pacific, the U.S. began its counteroffensive at Guadalcanal.

Guadalcanal

Growing Menace

During 1941–2, the Japanese had advanced from the Asian mainland into southeastern Asia, and the United States had to act to prevent them from threatening more of the region, including Australia and New Zealand. In August 1942, U.S. Marines landed on the occupied island of Guadalcanal.

> **Before Guadalcanal the enemy advanced at his pleasure—after Guadalcanal he retreated at ours.**
>
> *U.S. Admiral "Bull" Halsey*

The Kokoda Trail

While the U.S. attacked Guadalcanal, Australian troops fought off a bitter Japanese land assault in New Guinea. In a series of battles in which disease also claimed many lives, the outnumbered Australians were first pushed back along, and then reclaimed, the Kokoda Trail, a single-file path from the capital Port Moresby to the Solomon Sea. Had the Japanese succeeded, Australia itself may have faced invasion.

Hostile Terrain

The Marines found themselves in a land of mountains and ravines with no natural harbor to make use of. Meanwhile the Japanese, who were reinforcing daily, fought to the death rather than surrender. Only after weeks of fighting did the Marines establish a toehold on Guadalcanal, which allowed them to reinforce with army infantry. Expanding this conquest to the whole island would take months.

Hunger and Sickness

Yet the Japanese had problems too. A four-day naval battle in November wrecked their supply fleet and vastly reduced their capacity to reinforce. And both sides fell victim to disease in the humid climate. At one point, malaria was claiming five times more casualties among the U.S. troops than the conflict itself. But illness among the defending troops, combined with lack of supplies, allowed the Americans to win after a six-month campaign.

Lessons Learned

Capturing Guadalcanal was significant. For the first time, the United States had taken the offensive within captured Japanese territory. In doing so, it prevented Japan from controlling the entire Pacific, and received a grim foretaste of just how determined the Japanese were to defend their positions. The U.S. also gained valuable experience of fighting a shared campaign between their army, navy, and Marines. As the war continued, these lessons would prove their worth time and again.

Turning the South Pacific tide, 1942–3

May 8, 1942 End of Battle of Coral Sea.

July 29 Japanese capture Kokoda.

August 7 1942 U.S. invades Guadalcanal.

November 12-15 Naval battle of Guadalcanal.

February 8, 1943 Japanese begin withdrawal from Guadalcanal.

U.S. officers question a bewildered Japanese prisoner taken by the Marines during fighting in Guadalcanal in the Solomon Islands, November 11, 1942.

Stalingrad

Hitler's invasion of the Soviet Union was initially successful but later fell victim to dogged resistance and the fierce Russian winter. At Stalingrad, the Germans suffered their biggest reverse of all.

Stalingrad

> *In Stalingrad we see the reflection, as in a drop of water, of all the problems of the Nazis' predatory war.*
>
> General Friedrich Paulus

Zhukov: unsung Soviet hero

According to the Allied Supreme Commander, General Dwight Eisenhower, no one was owed more for Germany's defeat than the Soviet Marshal Georgi Zhukov. He fought—and won—epic battles at Moscow, Leningrad, Kursk, and Berlin, as well as Stalingrad. After the war, though, Zhukov was a victim of Stalin's jealousy. Official histories played down his achievements and later, as defense minister after Stalin's death, he was accused of political mistakes in running the military.

Prestigious Target

In spring 1942 Hitler launched two new offensives on the Eastern Front. One was a dash for the Caucasus oil reserves. The other was an assault on the city of Stalingrad (modernday Volgograd). This city, named after the Soviet leader himself, was of great symbolic importance. That summer, the German 6th Army under General Friedrich Paulus advanced on Stalingrad. Thousands of bombers and tanks pounded the city, and Nazi soldiers reached the banks of the River Volga, on which it was built, by September.

No Surrender

By October, Paulus held most of Stalingrad. But he could not make it submit. With streets so badly bombed that German tanks were of little use, the battle descended into vicious hand-to-hand fighting among the rubble. The Soviet Red Army—ordered by Stalin to defend at all costs—reinforced from east of the Volga and inflicted substantial casualties. But it was also building up a massive reserve to counterattack.

The Soviet Trap

In November, Hitler diverted hundreds of planes to his ailing North Africa campaign, weakening the Stalingrad front. That very month, the Red Army launched a huge assault led by one million soldiers. This overwhelmed the Romanian troops manning Paulus's supply lines, and soon, the 6th Army was stranded. As a ferocious winter closed in, the Germans suffered appalling hardship. Hitler though, forbade retreat. The Luftwaffe tried airlifting supplies to the stricken troops, but another big Soviet attack captured its airfields. Finally, faced with starvation or total destruction, Paulus ignored Hitler's orders and surrendered.

The Eastern Front, 1941–3

June 22, 1941 Operation Barbarossa—Germany invades the USSR.

September 19 Fall of Kiev.

November 23 German advance stalls, short of Moscow.

May 8, 1942 German offensive resumes after bitter winter.

August 23 6th Army reaches the Volga.

19 November Soviet counter-attack.

23 November 6th Army trapped at Stalingrad.

31 January 1943 Paulus surrenders.

Russian soldiers fight in the ruins of Stalingrad.

The Battle of Monte Cassino

In July 1943 Hitler's collaborator, the Italian dictator Benito Mussolini, was deposed.
It seemed a perfect opportunity for the Allies to invade Italy. But the difficulties of this plan soon became clear.

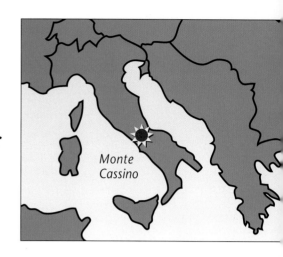

Monte Cassino

The Road to Rome

Progress in Italy was slow and German resistance was extremely strong. U.S. forces were led by General Mark Clark (below). The son of an infantry colonel, he became the youngest three-star general ever in October 1942.
Despite his troops liberating Rome in 1944, Clark's style of command was questioned by some who felt he had let the German army escape.

The Gustav Line

According to Churchill, Italy was Hitler's "soft underbelly"—ideal territory from which to invade Nazi Germany. After Mussolini's fall, the Allies made their way up the Italian peninsula to do just this. But the Germans swiftly occupied northern and central Italy, including Rome, and by the winter of 1943 the two sides faced each other over the so-called Gustav Line at Monte Cassino, south of the capital. This mountain, crowned with a Benedictine monastery, gave the Nazis a perfect defense.

Anzio

The Allies could not simply smash through the Gustav Line, so they hatched a plan to bypass it. An attack south of Monte Cassino would distract the enemy, while troops went by sea to skirt around the German lines. This first battle of Monte Cassino began in January 1944, and U.S. forces landed on the Italian coast at Anzio. However, rather than advancing they chose to secure the beach first, giving the Germans time to organize. When they did attack later, they met fierce resistance.

Immovable Enemy

The second battle began in the middle of February, and saw the Allies bomb the monastery, believing that it was being used to defend the mountain. It was not. However, its ruins did offer the Germans extra cover, and they remained in place.

Breakthrough

It was only with the third battle, commencing in the middle of March, that the stalemate was broken. The British 8th Army was brought in, along with the Free French infantry who defied German invulnerability by breaking through the Gustav Line. Meanwhile, Polish forces took Monte Cassino itself. By May the Germans were, at last, in full retreat, and Rome was liberated on June 4.

Allied Troubles

The Allies' difficulties in Italy were caused by several problems. First, the Italian countryside was an unforgiving battleground. More worrying were the differences that emerged between Allied military leaders in the field. The overall commander, General Alexander, lacked control, leaving some of his units effectively pursuing different objectives. Lessons would have to be learned if the more ambitious plans to invade France were to succeed.

The war in Italy, 1943–4

July 10, 1943 Allies invade Sicily.

July 25 Mussolini deposed.

September 3 Allies land on the Italian mainland.

January 22, 1944 Anzio landings.

May 18 Capture of Monte Cassino.

June 4 U.S. troops enter Rome.

A U.S. landing craft unloads at Anzio.

D-Day and the Battle for Normandy

By the spring of 1944, Hitler's dream of supremacy was in ruins, and Germany itself was threatened. So when the Allies invaded occupied France, they faced a desperate army, fighting for its life.

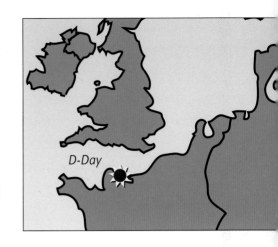

D-Day

Normandy's floating harbors

Normandy's harbors were heavily defended, so the invading Allies brought two of their own—in kit form. These "Mulberry" harbors consisted of huge concrete cubes that were floated into place and submerged. Ships unloaded at connecting piers, mounted on stilts, which could rise and fall with the tide. The Mulberry harbors were an ingenious technical feat, although one was destroyed in a storm.

Liberators From across the Sea

Planned for over a year, the invasion of Normandy in northern France was the biggest amphibious (water-borne) operation ever. On June 6, 1944 (D-Day), 156,000 men crossed the English Channel from Britain, landing on five beaches code-named Omaha, Utah, Gold, Juno, and Sword. Numerous tanks, guns, and supplies also had to be brought ashore. D-Day itself was only the start as thousands more men and weapons joined the invasion in the following weeks.

Into the Gunfire

Hitler expected an invasion, but the Allies deceived him into thinking it would happen 150 miles (240km) away, at Calais. Therefore, many German units were elsewhere and the Allies also enjoyed air superiority and could bomb the Germans as they maneuvered. Yet D-Day was no pushover. The troops landed on beaches strung with minefields and tank traps, and braved a storm of German bullets. On Omaha beach, the Americans suffered particularly severe losses. Altogether, 3,000 Allied men were killed on D-Day alone, and another 9,000 injured.

An aerial view of a "Mulberry" harbor.

Soldiers wade ashore during the Normandy landings.

Onward to Victory

Once the Allies were ashore, they had an equally tough battle to move inland. Normandy's countryside, with its hedges and winding lanes, favored the defenders. Allied casualties were on a scale rarely seen since the trench warfare of World War I. Yet there was no alternative to fighting on. Eventually, British and Canadian forces pinned down the Germans at Caen. Though this almost completely destroyed the town, it enabled American troops to break through the German lines. After that, the Allies made rapid progress through northern France, liberating Paris in August. The stage was set for the Nazis' final downfall, which came with Hitler's suicide in April 1945 and the surrender of Germany on May 7.

End of the Nazis, 1944–5

June 6, 1944 D-Day landings.

June 22 New Russian offensive, Operation Bagration.

July 20 German officers fail to assassinate Hitler.

September 26 Allies retreat at Arnhem, Holland.

August 25 Paris liberated by Allies.

December 17 Surprise German counter-attack. Later fails.

January 12, 1945 New Russian winter offensive savages the Germans from the East.

February 14 Allied bombers destroy Dresden.

April 30 Hitler commits suicide as Russians seize Berlin.

May 7 Germany surrenders unconditionally.

The Battle of Okinawa

By April 1945, the war in Europe was almost over as Germany crumbled. But in the Pacific, the Japanese held out at all costs against the U.S. forces. The result was a bloodbath.

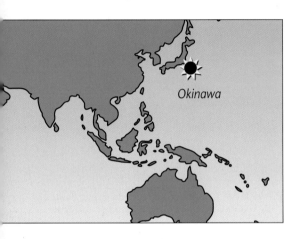

A defeated Japanese soldier staggers from a bunker on Okinawa.

Dawn of the nuclear age

The atom bombs dropped on Hiroshima and Nagasaki completely destroyed both cities, but some in Japan still wanted to fight on. It took Emperor Hirohito himself to bring about their surrender. The development of nuclear weapons helped the United States emerge from the war as a superpower. Yet German scientists had been experimenting, too. Had the Allies been less fortunate, Hitler might have got the bomb first.

Long Haul

Even as Germany faced defeat, an Allied assault on Japan seemed far off. The U.S. planned an invasion, but it was not due to start until November 1945—its final phase later still. To capture advance bases for this offensive, 50,000 American troops landed on the Japanese island of Okinawa on April 1.

Overwhelming Force

Backed up by warships, the Americans faced little opposition at first. Instead, the Japanese dug in. As a result, while the Americans took northern and central Okinawa relatively quickly, in the south they faced some of the most savage hand-to-hand combat of the war. Trapped Japanese units jumped off cliffs, or ran amok, preferring honorable death to surrender.

Kamikazes

As the Americans fought doggedly on, their casualty rate soared. In the waters around Okinawa, *kamikazes* (suicide planes) targeted U.S. ships. Eventually the U.S. lost 34 ships to these attacks, with hundreds more damaged. The far south of Okinawa saw some of the most stubborn resistance of all. Here, the Japanese hid in caves from which they could pick off the invaders. The Americans had to burn them out using flamethrowers. Finally, after 82 days of fighting, they captured the Japanese command cave on June 21, 1945.

Never Again

The battle was over, but the Americans had been forced to kill nearly all their enemy—at least 90,000 men. Only 7,000 surrendered. Up to 100,000 civilians also died, while the Americans themselves lost more than 12,000 lives. The carnage was so great that the plan to invade Japan's mainland later that year was scrapped for fear of even greater losses. Instead, the Americans now decided to defeat Japan with a new and utterly devastating weapon—the atom bomb. This killed tens of thousands at Hiroshima and Nagasaki. Japan was forced to surrender, ending the war.

Defeat of Japan, 1945

June 8 Japanese government vows to fight the war "until the bitter end."

June 21 U.S. forces finally subdue Okinawa.

June 28 U.S. liberates the Philippines.

July 16 U.S. tests its first atom bomb.

August 6 First atom bomb dropped on Hiroshima. 60,000 die instantly.

August 8 Soviet Union declares war on Japan.

August 9 Atom bomb dropped on Nagasaki.

August 15 Emperor Hirohito announces Japan's surrender.

> ❝ *We have used it in order to shorten the agony of war, in order to save the lives of thousands and thousands of young Americans.* ❞
>
> U.S. President Harry S. Truman, speaking about the atom bomb

Surveying the devastation: a survivor looks out over what once was Hiroshima after the city was destroyed by an atomic bomb.

Glossary

Allies The United States, Britain, Canada, the Soviet Union, and the other countries who fought against Germany, Italy, and Japan.

Appeasement A policy practiced by Britain and France before World War II, designed to avoid war by agreeing to German demands for territory and weapons.

Axis Germany, Italy, and later Japan formed the Axis powers, who fought together against the Allies.

Battleship The most powerful warship before the arrival of the aircraft carrier.

Civilian A woman or man who is an ordinary citizen rather than a member of the armed forces.

Communism A political ideology that claims to create equality between social classes by using the state to take over the economy.

ENIGMA The secret code used by Germany to communicate with its military units. The code was broken and known to the Allies throughout most of the war.

Fascism Authoritarian rule pioneered in Italy by Mussolini, and characterized by extreme nationalism, anticommunism, and adoration for the country's leader.

Ghetto In medieval times, the part of a city to which Jews were restricted. The Nazis recreated ghettoes in order to imprison and isolate Jews from the population at large.

Hitler, Adolf (1889–1945) Nazi leader and dictator of Germany after 1933. Hitler demanded absolute loyalty and had an obsessive hatred of Jews.

Kamikaze Japanese suicide pilot who used his plane as a missile, usually against a U.S. warship.

Lebensraum German for "living space"—Hitler's term for the extra land he wanted to conquer in eastern Europe.

Luftwaffe The German air force.

Nazi Member of Hitler's National Socialist Party, which advocated German racial supremacy and the destruction of Jewish influence.

Neutrality The policy of not fighting or taking sides in a conflict.

Radar Device using radio waves to detect the location and direction of enemy aircraft or ships. Stands for "radio detection and ranging."

Radio silence Method of avoiding detection by not using radio communications.

Soviet Union (USSR) The name sometimes used to describe Russia under communism, but more correctly, the wider union of communist republics governed from Moscow. Also known as the USSR (Union of Soviet Socialist Republics).

Sudetenland German-speaking region of Czechoslovakia, ceded to Germany under prewar appeasement policy.

Supply lines The routes by which an army is supplied with food, ammunition etc. Long supply lines can become very difficult to protect.

Total war The mobilization of a country's entire population and economy in order to wage war.

U-boat A German submarine.

WEB SITES

www.spartacus.schoolnet.co.uk/2WW.htm
   A comprehensive site covering every aspect of World War II, including both the military campaigns and the home front.

www.bbc.co.uk/history/worldwars/wwtwo/
   The official BBC site on the war, with numerous photographs, maps, and spoken word extracts.

www.historyplace.com/worldwar2/timeline/ww2time.htm
   A detailed timeline of events from 1918 to the end of World War II, with many photographs.

Index